Essential ~~Oils~~
&
Handy Tips
for the home & garden

Essential Hints
&
Handy Tips
for the home & garden

Lucy Doncaster
& Karen Farrington

HOTHOUSE

HOTHOUSE

This book was first published in 2004 in Great Britain
by Igloo Books Ltd., Henson Way, Telford Way Industrial Estate,
Kettering, Northants NN16 8PX
hothouse@igloo-books.com

This book was created for Igloo Books
by Amazon Publishing Ltd., 7 Old Lodge Place, Twickenham,
Middlesex, TW1 1QR

Authors Lucy Doncaster and Karen Farrington
Editor Mary Davies
Designer Maggie Aldred

ISBN 1-84561-003-2
Printed and bound in China

Foreword

As gardening and home maintenance become more popular, there is an ever greater appetite for household and horticultural know-how and advice. This rise in popularity has been matched by an increased environmental awareness, which in turn has led to a greater emphasis on the use of natural techniques over harsher chemical alternatives wherever possible. This book aims to provide clear, accessible guidelines incorporating this more environmentally aware mode of thinking, in order to produce green tips suitable for the budding novice, weathered gardener and housekeepers of all ages. Tips have been collated from a wide range of sources – mostly, of course, from experienced housewives and gardeners – but also from books, magazines and the internet. Please note, it is important that due caution is taken when using chemicals, products and techniques outlined in this book, and their success cannot be guaranteed. All treatments should be tested prior to application, in an inconspicuous place, and please read and follow all information on product labels with care.

Contents

GARDEN
Hints and Tips
102

HOUSEHOLD
Hints and Tips

*We all enjoy living in a clean, well-ordered household,
but achieving and maintaining this ideal is often
time consuming and tiring. This book aims
to provide you with a few pointers for dealing with
even the most taxing problems and help you breeze
your way to housekeeping brilliance.*

Stain Removal

Stains occur in every household, and, if left untreated, can be a permanent reminder of dinner parties, sporting accidents or muddy walks past. So try these spot-on solutions to leave your laundry, shoes upholstery and carpets as unblemished as your reputation.

First Aid

Different stains require different treatments according to the type of the fabric, but here are some general points about the immediate action you should take.

The quicker you deal with stains the better. The first step should always be to try and absorb as much of the fluid, or remove as much of the substance, as possible.

If the fabric is dry-clean only, you should rub the stain immediately with an ice cube rather than a cloth as this prevents the stain from setting and avoids damaging delicate fibres.

Wherever possible, try to deal with stains on the reverse of the fabric to prevent them sinking in further. You should always work the solution towards the centre to prevent it spreading.

Salt absorbs stains and is often the best immediate action to take on spills such as red wine and beetroot.

You should never use warm water to treat protein stains, such as egg or blood, as heat will seal in the stain.

If the fabric is washable, check the label to see what temperature the material can withstand.

Clothes

It is often hard to avoid getting stains on clothes, and children in particular are prone to picking up a variety of different marks, ranging from grass, chocolate and grease to ink, blood and paint. Here are some handy ways to erase the tell-tale marks of everyday accidents.

Acrylic paint
Rub the area with soap and cold water,
and then again with methylated spirit, before washing as usual.

Beetroot
Cover the area repeatedly with salt or press the stain between two slices of dampened bread until all of the fluid is absorbed. Alternatively, plunge clothes immediately into cold water before rubbing with liquid detergent. If it is a material like cotton which won't be spoilt by heat, douse the area with boiling water until it runs clear.

Blood

Put the garment into a bucket of cold salty water or a solution of
hydrogen peroxide and water in a ration of 1:3 as quickly as possible.
If the blood has dried, then remove any 'crusting' and soak
in cold water with biological detergent before washing as usual.

Chewing gum

Put the article in the freezer for an hour, crack the gum off,
rub the mark with distilled vinegar or egg white, and wash.

Chocolate, coffee and cocoa

For non-delicates, stretch the fabric taut over a bowl, sprinkle
with borax powder and pour boiling water through the stain.
Then soak the item in the solution for an hour before washing.
For more delicate materials, dab the mark with glycerine and leave
for 15 minutes before washing according to recommendations
on the label.

Curry
Hold the stain under warm running water until the
water runs clear, then dab with glycerine and leave overnight
before soaking in biological detergent and washing.

Deodorant
Make a paste of bicarbonate of soda, salt and water
or some glycerine, apply to the affected area
and leave for 15 minutes. Then soak in biological detergent
and water and finally wash.

Fat/grease
Remove as much of the substance as possible, then
carefully blot the area with kitchen towel or brown paper.
Apply baking soda or talcum powder to draw up the grease
and leave for 10 minutes before applying some spray lubricant, such as
WD40, followed 10 minutes later by washing-up liquid. Then wash.

Foundation
Dab with liquid detergent and then rinse.

Fruit juice

Blot the area with kitchen paper to absorb as
much of the stain as possible. If the item is not silk, soak in lemon
juice for 30 minutes and then launder as usual. For silk, blot dry, then
sponge on some distilled vinegar, rinse with cool water and dry-clean.

Grass

Rub nylon with glycerine and leave for an hour before
laundering. For other materials, use methylated spirits and then
rinse with warm water before washing.

Hair dye

Put the item straight into cold water, and then rub with
liquid detergent followed by distilled vinegar.

Ink

The quickest and easiest way to remove ink blotches is to
coat the area in hairspray and let it dry before laundering.
Alternatively, you can rub the spots with a cut lemon and sprinkle
with salt, or rub in a paste made from milk and baking soda
before rinsing and washing.

Lipstick

Rub with methylated spirits, glycerine or petroleum jelly before washing in a 20:1 solution of liquid detergent and ammonia.

Perfume

Rub the area with a 1:1 dilution of water and glycerine before rinsing and laundering as usual.

Perspiration

For recent stains, soak the item in 2.5ml ammonia with 1 litre warm water for half an hour, or apply a paste of baking soda and water and leave overnight. On older stains, dab with neat distilled vinegar and leave for 2 hours.

Plasticine ™

Rub with a clean cloth and lighter fuel and then wash in hot water, or warm water if the garment is made from a delicate material.

Red wine

Apply salt repeatedly until it no longer absorbs wine, or cover the area with white wine, before washing as usual.

Rust

Cover the area with salt and add a few drops of
lemon juice. Leave it for half an hour, preferably in the sun,
and then rinse in a solution of 25ml ammonia
per 10 litres of water before washing.

Salad dressing/mayonnaise

Rub with glycerine and then wash in a mild solution of
25ml ammonia and 10 litres of warm water.

Scorch marks

To remove from white fabric, dampen a clean
cloth with hydrogen peroxide and place it over
the stain, put another clean cloth over the top and
gently warm with an iron.

Tea

For recent spills, soak in a solution of 500ml warm
water and 15ml borax. For older spills, try rubbing with
glycerine or methylated spirits.

Urine

Soak the item in a 6:1 dilution of water and
hydrogen peroxide, with a few drops of ammonia
added. Launder as normal.

White wine

Cover in salt until all the liquid is absorbed and then rinse
with cold water before washing as instructed.

Water-based paint

Rinse in cold water or dab with neat ammonia
before washing.

Carpets and Upholstery

**Carpets and upholstery undergo a lot of wear
and tear, and have to withstand all manner of spills
and accidents. Here are some on-the-spot
suggestions to help banish the blots.**

Burns

Use fine sandpaper to remove most of the burnt fibres and then
trim away any remaining with nail scissors. If it is a carpet burn
in an obvious place, trim some fibres (or a square of carpet if the burn
is large) from a patch of carpet which is hidden, for example by a
piece of furniture, and glue into the hole.

Faded colour

Scatter a mixture of tea leaves and salt over the carpet
before vacuuming.

Grease spots

On rugs, rub with a 1:4 dilution of salt and alcohol.
Alternatively, treat the area with paint thinner or lighter fuel,
and then blot, rather than rub, with kitchen paper.

Maintenance

Regular hoovering helps to maintain the condition of your
carpets as well as improving the appearance of the room.
Vacuum the upholstery once a fortnight too, and try to keep it
out of direct sunlight as this fades the colours.

Mildew or mould

Lightly spray porous upholstery fabric with a 1:1 solution
of tea tree oil and water and then air as much as possible.
If the material is non-porous, use borax or vinegar
instead of tea tree oil.

Muddy patches

Freshen discoloured areas on carpets by
rinsing with water left over from boiling potatoes.

Odours

Sprinkle the carpet with bicarbonate of soda and leave
for 30 minutes before vacuuming.

Rust marks

On carpets and rugs, treat the area with a 1:4 solution of salt and alcohol, rubbing in the direction of the nap.

Scorch marks

Rub the area with a raw onion or potato.

Spills

Salt soaks up most spills – in particular red wine and ink. Apply salt repeatedly until it won't absorb any more liquid, before letting it dry and vacuuming.

Stains

On dark-coloured carpets, rub ground coffee into the affected area before vacuuming.

Treat stubborn stains by gently scrubbing the area with shaving cream and a scrubbing brush after blotting with paper towels.

Shoes

Shoes and trainers inevitably become scuffed and dirty, and if left untreated can look scruffy. Luckily, there are many effective ways to produce smart results that can help to prolong life too.

Black marks
Rub with nail polish remover or lighter fuel.

Have a banana
Rubbing leather shoes with the soft inside of a banana skin cleans and polishes at the same time.

Instant shine
In a hurry? Rub your leather shoes with a baby-wipe. But don't do this too often as baby-wipes can dry the leather out. Be sure to clean and polish the shoes properly soon afterwards.

Mud

Leave shoes or trainers on a piece of newspaper outside or
in an airing cupboard before scraping off the worst of the dirt.
It's so much easier to remove once dry.

Odours

Chop the toe off an old pair of tights and fill it with
cat litter, baking soda or tea leaves. Place in the offending
shoes when they are not in use.

Patent leather

Store shoes in a warm place and rub with milk or olive oil
every once in a while to prevent cracking.

Scuffs

For a smooth, unblemished surface, fill scratches and scuffs by rubbing
a raw potato over the affected area before applying polish.

Suede

Rub with a little lemon juice, steam for a few seconds over
a kettle and then brush with a suede brush. A pencil eraser will
remove grease marks.

Waterproofing

For leather, apply a thin, even coat of castor oil.

Wet shoes

Place chopped conkers in saturated shoes – it dries them out.

White leather

Apply cleansing milk with cotton wool before buffing
with a soft cloth.

Laundry

Have your whites lost their glow? Does the thought of washing

your woollens or starching you shirts fill you with horror?

Fear no longer — these laundry lifesavers will make drying

a doddle and washday a breeze.

Caring For Woollens

**Delicate woollens require special treatment,
so try these skin-friendly tips to ensure safe
washing for soft woollens.**

Always use lukewarm water when washing delicate woollens.
Extreme temperatures shock the fibres and can cause
them to shrink.

For extra-soft woollens, add a little distilled vinegar to
the final rinse. It helps to wash out every last trace of soap.

When handwashing, avoid dunking the garment in
and out of the water as this stretches the wool, and press in a
towel to remove excess water rather than wringing.

Hair shampoo and conditioner can be used to clean and
condition delicate fibres such as mohair, angora and cashmere.
Add a small blob of conditioner to the final rinse,
after hand washing with shampoo, and it will help to untangle
matted fibres and soften the fabric, as well as preventing static
and gently perfuming the garment. These products are particularly
suitable for those with sensitive skin – what is suitable
for the scalp, should be suitable for the rest of the body.

If you don't have time to handwash delicates such as cashmere,
it's good idea to put them into a net bag or pillow case with the end
tied up. This prevents them snagging in the washing machine.

To avoid peg marks when you hang less delicate woollens on the line,
try threading an old pair of tights through the sleeves and pegging
that to the line, rather than the actual garment.

If you have a snag in a woollen garment, pull the loop
through to the inside with a sewing or knitting
needle (depending on the chunkiness of the wool).
Never cut the loop as this will cause
the stitches to unravel.

Rubbing matted mohair with a piece of Velcro™ will
restore a garment to its former fluffiness.

Use hair conditioner to restore shape to clothes
which have shrunk. Simply soak the article in a solution of warm
water and conditioner for 30 minutes, before gently stretching
and reshaping while damp.

Blinding Whites

Clean, crisp, bright whites are always a pleasure to wear, so here are some easy ways to restore your laundry to its brilliant best.

For dazzling whites, try mixing a teaspoon of baking soda with your washing powder before you put it in the machine. This also helps to eliminate lingering tobacco odours.

Add a mixture of 1 tablespoon methylated spirit and 1 tablespoon turpentine to the final rinse of your wash to prevent whites yellowing.

Place a linen bag containing crushed egg shells in your machine with the load to help whiten the grubbiest garments.

Lemon is a natural bleaching agent and can be used on
most white fabrics apart from silk. Soak the soiled item in a
bucket of boiling water mixed with 100ml (3½ fl.oz) of lemon juice
or a few slices of lemon for at least 30 minutes and then
launder as normal.

Make a delicate bleach solution suitable for whitening woollens by
mixing 3% hydrogen peroxide with water, at a dilution of 1:8.

Line-drying sheets and other white linens on a sunny day
not only freshens but also brightens them.

...and to keep whites white

Test new coloureds for fastness by soaking a small area with warm
water and squeezing. If the dye runs, it's best to wash the garment
on its own. And remember: always wash pale
and dark colours separately.

Line-Fresh Linen

**Fresh linen straight from the line has a wonderful scent,
but unfortunately this rarely lasts, so try these simple tricks
to maintain the freshness long beyond laundry day.**

To add a hint of your favourite perfume to your underwear,
put a few drops to the final rinse.

When washing a blanket, add a bath cube or a few drops of essential
oil to the final rinse for lasting scent. This is particularly effective
when the blankets have not been used for a while.

Lightly fragrance your clothes by misting them with a lavender
and water solution before you iron them.

Old handkerchiefs can quickly be turned into scent pouches for chests and drawers by placing some of your favourite aromatic herbs and flowers, such as lavender or rosemary, in the centre, before twisting and tying with a ribbon.

Fabric-conditioning sheets are obtainable from most supermarkets. Used ones, placed in chests and drawers, help to maintain freshness.

Starching and Ironing

Crisp collars and cuffs are always a confidence booster, and careful starching and ironing improves the appearance of any fabric, especially if it has become limp through multiple washes. But did you know starch also helps to repel dirt and grime? These tips will help you to steam through your ironing with ease.

Add starch to the final cycle of your wash to avoid the hassle of applying starch to each article individually.

Iron collars from the points inwards. It helps to prevent rucking and creasing.

Don't let the iron become too hot when pressing a starched item. It can cause the starch to flake off.

You can make your own starch by mixing 2 teaspoons
of cornstarch with 1 litre of water. Put it in a spray
bottle and use while ironing.

If you accidentally iron-in a crease, simply dab the area with a damp
sponge or spray with some water and iron smooth.

Steam vents on irons can become blocked, especially if you
use starch frequently. Try filling the iron with distilled vinegar and
either switch it on and leave for 20 minutes or press the steam
function repeatedly until the nozzles are clear. Then disconnect
the iron, tip away any remaining vinegar and rinse out.

Don't iron fabric while it's wet enough to cause the iron
to hiss. It may result in scorching.

To get rid of grease marks around collars and cuffs, rub
the areas with a stick of chalk and leave overnight
before washing.

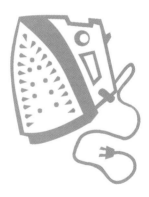

Kitchen

Are you tired of the endless cycle of soak and scrub?

Are you unknowingly aiding and abetting dangerous germs?

Kitchens are areas which require constant attention, so here

are some tidy tricks to ensure a squeaky clean sheen.

Useful Utensils

With the bewildering amount of gadgets on sale it is easy to spend money on unnecessary and expensive items which create clutter. Here are some useful ways to get the same result using existing, everyday kitchen implements.

Ceramic baking beans are not particularly expensive, but if you are not going to use them very often then dried beans or rice work just as well.

A hand-held beater mashes potatoes much better than individual potato mashers and can be used for many more purposes besides.

An ordinary new paint brush is just as good as a 'pastry brush' and will probably be cheaper.

Kitchen paper or a clean tea towel are more effective for drying off rinsed salad leaves than a cumbersome salad spinner.

The plastic tubs that takeaway curries and ready-made sauces come in make very effective storage tubs, especially for freezing and storing smaller quantities. Because they may not be airtight, it's better not to use them for biscuits and cakes. NB Do not put in the oven and always check whether they are suitable for the microwave.

Wearing washing-up gloves, or placing an elastic band around the lid, to open a stiff jar works just as well as a jar-opening gadget.

To keep the inside of your kettle clean, drop in an old oyster shell which will prevent limescale building up.

Egg slicers can be used to cut mushrooms and soft fruits, such as kiwi, strawberries and bananas.

You can easily make café-quality frothy milk for cappuccinos and hot chocolate at home without an expensive gadget. Simply heat the milk in a pan and whisk with a hand-held beater.

Pristine Pans

We all know how frustrating it can be when stubbon stains refuse to shift, so here are some environmentally friendly ways to keep your pans gleaming.

Never put uncoated aluminium pans in a dishwasher.
The metal will react with the detergent and tarnish.

Restore stained copper pots and pans to their
spotless best by dipping half a lemon in salt and rubbing
the marks with a circular motion.

Remove black tarnish from aluminium or stainless steel
cookware by covering the base of the pan with slices of lemon
and water and boiling for 30 minutes.

For badly burned-on food, soak in water for an
hour, and then boil with a chopped onion and a tablespoon of
salt for another hour.

Another good method to try for severe burnt-on stains, is to boil
a solution of 1 litre of water and 1 tablespoon of biological detergent
in the pan for 10 minutes.

Remove hard-water marks from stainless steel pans by
bringing some water and 4 tablespoons of distilled vinegar to
the boil in them, and then cleaning with a nylon scourer.

Don't be tempted to plunge very hot cookware into
water to make cleaning easier. Cookware can warp if it is too
hot when you wash it, so leave it to cool for 10 minutes.

Never use metal implements or wire wool on non-stick coating
– even to remove burnt-on grime. Instead, bring 125ml water and
2 tablespoons of baking soda up to the boil in the pan, then rinse
and dry thoroughly. Alternatively, use a nylon scrubbing brush or pad.

To lengthen the life of a non-stick coating, 'season' the pan
after drying by wiping the inside with some vegetable or olive oil.

To prevent non-stick cookware from becoming scratched
while stacked, place old plastic yoghurt or cream pot
lids between each pan after drying.

Spotless Surfaces

**Kitchen surfaces can be breeding grounds
for bacteria and need regular wiping, but sometimes
conventional cleaning just doesn't leave them
pristine. Here are some other ways to achieve
the cleanest sheen.**

Sterilise your sponges and avoid spreading germs when
wiping surfaces by putting them through the dishwasher
with the day's load.

To lift stains from formica surfaces, cover the area with
lemon juice and leave for 30 minutes before rubbing with
bicarbonate of soda and wiping clean.

Keep wooden surfaces clean by scrubbing with scouring powder
before rubbing in a little olive oil to build up a seal.

Use silicone furniture polish on wooden surfaces in the kitchen rather than wax, which traps grease and softens the surface.

Rub a little non-gel toothpaste onto a plastic worksurface before buffing with a soft cloth to ensure a gleamingly clean result.

To remove rust and water spots from stainless-steel sinks, apply distilled vinegar or alcohol with a sponge or soft cloth.

Rejuvenate dull sinks by wetting paper towels with bleach, pressing them onto the affected surface and leaving for a couple of hours. Then rinse thoroughly.

Clean Cookers and Hobs

Spills are an almost inevitable part of cooking, but they can be tricky to shift and leave your cooker and hob smoking and looking dirty. Try these traditional techniques instead.

Pour salt over recent liquid spills while the oven is on to prevent smoking. When it is turned off and cool, you'll be able to lift the spill easily.

To prevent food from sticking to your cooker top when pans spill over, try rubbing some car wax or distilled vinegar on the surface occasionally after cleaning.

Place a saucer of water containing a few drops of distilled vinegar in the microwave and turn it on for 2 minutes. It will help to remove cooked-on spills and deodorize at the same time.

Remove melted plastic from a hob or oven top by letting it cool and harden before you apply nail-varnish remover. Leave for 10 minutes and then wipe off with a soft, dry cloth.

Clear blocked vents on gas hobs quickly and easily with a pipe cleaner dipped in washing-up liquid.

Use a disposable razor to lift crusty spills and you won't scratch the surface.

Remove marks on stainless-steel ovens with a little baby oil.

Don't want to use chemical solvents on your oven? Try using a 1:4 mixture of borax and baking soda as scouring powder.

To get rid of the smell of a commercial oven-cleaner, put
half a lemon in a hot oven and leave for 15 minutes with the door
shut, followed by 10 minutes with the door ajar.

To remove burnt-on food stains from a cooker, soak any
removable parts overnight in a solution of warm water and
biological washing detergent, or mix the same ingredients into
a paste and apply directly to the surface.

Tackle heavy, greasy soiling on your cooker top or oven by applying
full-strength ammonia to the area, covering with foil and leaving it for
as long as possible with the extractor fan on or the windows open.
To deal with the inside of the oven, simply leave a cup containing 1ml
ammonia and 50ml water overnight, with the oven on its lowest
temperature setting. Remember you must wear rubber gloves
and keep pets and children away when dealing with ammonia.

Cupboards and Floors

Hygiene is vital in the kitchen, and while most people wipe surfaces regularly, floors and cupboards can often be overlooked. Here are some effective ways to combat grimy floors and sticky shelves.

Loose vinyl floor tiles in the kitchen are both a hazard and a haven for breeding bacteria. If the tiles are undamaged, gently heat them with a warm iron to melt the glue – you'll need the iron set to synthetics and a folded cloth to protect the surface. Lift the tiles, and scrape the old adhesive off the floor before applying fresh glue to the tiles and replacing. If the tiles are damaged, you'll need to put new ones down.

To ensure that the cloth you use to clean floors or shelves is sterile, and avoid spreading germs, put the dampened cloth into the microwave for 1 minute on full power.

Remove black scuffmarks from a white vinyl floor with a
pencil rubber, or try rubbing the marks with toothpaste.

Banish stains from lino with very fine wire wool and turpentine,
before polishing with a 1:1 mixture of milk and water.

When cleaning a vinyl floor, always sweep or hoover the area
first, before mopping with a weak solution of warm water and borax
or distilled vinegar to maintain shine as you clean.

Add some bicarbonate of soda to your bucket of hot
soapy water when cleaning the floor or cupboards. This will help
to shift the greasiest of grime.

If your wooden floorboards are creaking, dust some
talcum powder over the joins.

If you have a wooden kitchen floor, add a couple of
teabags to warm water and wipe the surface with a mop dampened
with the solution. This not only cleans but also disguises
scratches and flaws.

Rather than spending ages scrubbing the insides of cupboards, line
them with old newspaper. Then all you have to do is simply discard
the old paper and lay down fresh sheets.

Store bags of sugar and flour in outer plastic bags, or empty them into sealed jars rather than keeping them just in their original wrappings. This helps to ensure that cupboard surfaces don't become sticky or dusty. Keeping sugary items in sealed containers also helps to prevent insects being attracted to the kitchen.

The bottom of pans and baking trays can become greasy if the oven and hobs are not cleaned regularly. To avoid transferring the grime from cooker to cupboard, or from the bottom of one pan to the inside of another if they are stacked, make sure you wash the bottoms of pans as carefully as the insides.

Cupboard and drawer handles are breeding grounds for germs because bacteria is transferred from our hands to them whenever we use them. Include them in your regular cleaning regime and wipe with disinfectant every time you clean the surfaces.

Around the Home

Homes can house all manner of grime, pests, smells and mess, all of which draw the eye and damage the appearance, ambience and often the sanitation of the area. Wherever you are in the home, try these easy ways to defy the dust, prevent the pest and outwit the odour.

Natural Pest Prevention

**Ants, silverfish, flies and mice are just some of
the pests found in the kitchen, and they need to be dealt
with quickly and efficiently. But some modern methods
involve highly toxic ingredients not suitable for a
kitchen, especially if you have pets or children, so here
are some safer alternatives.**

If you don't want to use ant poison in the kitchen,
try dusting cinnamon or black pepper around the area where
the ants are entering your home. Chalk can also act as a deterrent so
draw a line across access points. Alternatively, ants are know to be
deterred by mint. Grow it near doorways or place a
few crushed leaves in entrances.

Are you unlucky enough to have a cockroach problem?
Place jam lids containing a mixture of sugar and borax in a 3:1 ratio
under sinks and behind the fridge, and sprinkle the mixture into
crevices which cannot be accessed by pets or small children.

Mosquitos breed around standing water so make sure it
can't collect anywhere just outside your home. If that's not the cause,
stick some cloves into a lemon and leave it near each window,
or put a saucer of clove oil in every room.

If your pet has fleas, put a couple of mothballs
in the bag of your vacuum cleaner – or dust-collection bin if your
machine is bagless – and vacuum daily for a week.
Then sprinkle garlic powder or iodized salt onto surfaces to kill any
fleas which may be lurking in your carpets or upholstery as well
as treating the animal by conventional means.

Hairspray is an effective and less toxic way of deterring flies
and bees than conventional insect sprays.

Lavender acts as both a deterrent to winged insects and as
a pleasant aroma in the home. Grow it just outside windows, keep
dried lavender in a bowl near windows, or use lavender
oil above an oil burner.

Basil and marigolds will deter winged insects and fleas,
and sprigs of fresh peppermint or camomile will deter mice, so keep
pots on windowsills or growing around doorways.

Dried lavender, elderflowers or chips of cedar wood will
deter moths and scent your fabrics. Put some in linen or cotton bags
– which can be made from old handkerchieves – and place them in
wardrobes and drawers.

Trap wasps or bees with some sweet liquid in a tall glass jar, put
the lid on once they have entered and release them outside.

Deter silverfish by keeping surfaces dry. If they do appear,
sprinkle some dampened cloths with powdered plaster and leave
overnight on surfaces upon which the silverfish been seen, before
shaking the cloth outside in the morning. Alternatively, put
a couple of cloves in drawers and cupboards.

Squirrels are a nuisance when they dig up bulbs from
window boxes and hanging baskets. Luckily they dislike
'cayenne hot' capsicum pepper, so sprinkle it on top of the soil
and on the window ledges to deter them.

Odour Prevention

**Fridges, bathrooms and bins can all smell a bit pungent,
especially in the summer months, but fortunately there are
many ways to avoid and combat the problem.**

The best way to stop your fridge smelling is to keep an eye
on the contents so they don't go rotten. Regular cleaning with a
solution of water and distilled vinegar will combat any existing smells
and give you the opportunity for a clear-out.

A jar filled with a 4:1 solution of cold water and bicarbonate
of soda at the back of your fridge will help to prevent smells.

To eliminate fridge odours, place half an apple, a lump
of charcoal, some slices of bread or some used coffee grounds
in an out-of-the-way corner.

Fridges sometimes smell because they're not shutting
properly. Test the seal by trapping a bank note in the door.
If you can pull it out, you need a new seal.

Remove fish odours from bins and surfaces by wiping with a
4:1 solution of water and bicarbonate of soda, or soda water.

To prevent the growth of bacteria and moulds which cause odours to
develop, sprinkle half a cup of borax in the bottom of your bin. For
maximum effectiveness, tip the old borax into the full bag and shake
fresh into the bottom of the bin each time you change the bag.

To help to deter insects as well as neutralize odours,
put a couple of mothballs in the bottom of your kitchen,
bathroom and wastepaper bins.

Do you have a waste-disposal unit in your sink that's
become blocked and smelly? Try dropping ice cubes and orange or
lemon peel down it, before flushing with cold water.

Pouring flat cola down your toilet bowl helps to shift limescale
and prevents odours from building up.

To clean a toilet bowl, drop in a couple of effervescent
stomach-upset tablets such as Alka Seltzer™, and leave for 30 minutes
before brushing and flushing.

Distilled vinegar or soda water can be used to banish urine smells in
the bathroom. Simply wipe the area with a cloth soaked in either
substance. For long-term odour prevention, place an old
yoghurt pot filled with cat litter in a corner.

Perfume and Potpourri

**A sweetly-scented room is a pleasure to occupy and
can enhance your sense of well-being, so here are some
quick tips to freshen any space.**

Dab a few drops of your favourite scent onto lightbulbs to ensure that
rooms are flooded with light and fragrance every time you turn
on the switch. Make sure the light has been off for a while before
applying the perfume – otherwise the bulbs may shatter.

To get rid of lingering tobacco smoke, place a bowl containing
1 tablespoon of lavender oil and 1ml ammonia mixed with 500ml
water in the room until the smell has gone.

Musty odours can be eliminated by regular airing, and, in the winter
months, by placing citrus peel on warm radiators around the home.

Scented flowers such as gardenias or roses will fill a room
with their natural scent, so plant them near a window or have
vases of cut flowers in your rooms.

Freshen the air in your home easily and naturally by
mixing some lemon juice with water, putting it in a spray bottle
and misting rooms each day.

To make your bathroom smell nice, mix 10 drops of your
favourite essential oil with some baking powder, sprinkle on the
bathroom mat, leave for an hour and then shake outside.

Make your own air-freshening tablets by mixing 125ml of salt,
125ml of flour and a few drops of essential oil together to form a
paste. Roll the paste into balls, using your hands, and leave to dry.
Place the dried balls in the corners of rooms.

Dusting and Polishing

**Dust-free, polished woodwork and ornaments
improve the look of any room. Here are some easy ways
to tackle the worst marks and tarnishes.**

Rub a water stain or scratch on woodwork with a shelled walnut
to help fill and disguise it. Alternatively, stain the scratch with
a little iodine and fill it in by rubbing the area with some
high-quality beeswax.

Eliminating some white water or heat rings on wooden surfaces
can be more difficult. If rubbing with a shelled walnut doesn't work,
try rubbing the area with a 1:1 paste of baking soda and non-gel
toothpaste followed by buffing with normal polish. Alternatively,
you could try rubbing the area with a cloth dabbed with vegetable oil
and then cigarette ash, or applying some real mayonnaise, leaving
it overnight, and then wiping clean with a dry cloth.

Make sure that your duster is made from cotton or flannel because synthetics can scratch the surface of many items.

Fabric-softener sheets help to repel dust so use one to wipe down the slats of your blinds after dusting.

To dust delicate items such as lampshades and ornaments, use a soft paintbrush. It will enable you to access all the nooks and crannies gently.

Televisions and electrical equipment become dusty very quickly because they produce static electricity and that attracts dust molecules. To combat the problem, wipe the item with a rag moistened with a 1:4 fabric conditioner and water solution, or use a fabric softening sheet.

You can dust hard-to-reach, narrow areas, such as
between a book shelf and a wall, by sliding a sock over the
end of a hanger and using that to clean.

Shine as you dust by using a cloth that has been soaked
in a mixture of 1 litre of water, two tablespoons of distilled vinegar
and four drops of lemon oil, before being wrung out. Once you
finish cleaning, keep the cloth in an jam jar with the lid
on to keep it moist.

Make your own wood polish by adding a few drops of
lemon juice to a 3:1 mixture of olive oil and distilled vinegar.
Apply to wooden surfaces with a sponge or mop according
to the area to be covered.

For brilliant brass, rub the article with half a lemon which has been
dipped with salt. This cleans and shines in one.

To clean heavily tarnished silverware, bring
2 teaspoons of salt, 2 teaspoons of bicarbonate of soda and 1 litre
of water to the boil in a pan with a piece of aluminium foil in
the bottom. Then place the silverware in the liquid, boil for
3 minutes and dry and polish with a soft cloth.

Glistening Glass

**Smudged, dirty glass and mirrors are a real
letdown, especially if they are on display, so here are
some top tips to make them shine.**

Crystal should always be handwashed – never put it in the
dishwasher. For an extra-clean gleam, wash it in a 1:3 solution
of distilled vinegar and water.

To clean glass vases and remove the odour which flower
stems can sometimes produce, half fill them with cold water,
add a tablespoon of mustard powder, stir and leave
for 30 minutes before rinsing.

Air freshener is a great alternative to window cleaner
for cleaning mirrors, and it makes it mirror smell fresh too.

Fill scratches on mirrors with a paste of non-gel toothpaste and silver polish, leave for 5 minutes and then buff off with a lint-free cloth.

For streak-free mirrors and glass surfaces, try using a solution of water and ammonia in a dilution of 10:1 and wiping with old newspaper.

To remove all traces of grime from a glass container, half fill it with water, add some peeled and grated potato and leave to soak for as long as possible. Alternatively, add a dash of vinegar, a handful of uncooked rice and a pinch of salt to the water in your container and swirl it around before rinsing.

Unused coffee filters are great for cleaning glass ornaments
and windows because they don't leave streaks.

When cleaning glass-fronted pictures, always spray
the cleaning solution onto the cloth rather than the glass itself, as
drips from direct spraying may seep under the
glass and spoil the picture.

Tiles and Taps

**Hard water and limescale can leave bathroom fixtures
and fittings dull and scaly, or, at worst, mildewed and slimy.
While there is no permanent solution, there are ways to
produce that clean sheen every time.**

A dampened cloth sprinkled with bicarbonate of soda
works wonders on porcelain tiles and sinks.

Shift rust and water spots on stainless-steel taps and fittings by
rubbing with lighter fuel or distilled vinegar.

For a lasting shine on dirty brass fittings, smear with brown
sauce and then polish with a cut lemon dipped in salt. Alternatively,
rub with a cloth dampened with white spirit.

Has your white bath become dull and marked with age?
Mix some turpentine with a teaspoon of salt and wipe it over
the whole surface before rinsing well with warm water.

Lift yellow stains underneath taps by applying a paste made of equal
amounts of salt and distilled vinegar. Leave it to work for 30 minutes.

Use a mixture of liquid laundry detergent and water to
clean the grime from bathtubs and tiles. It will also restore the
original brightness to tiles discoloured by hard water.

Baby oil acts as a barrier against limescale and soap scum when
rubbed onto wall tiles and shower screens (not the floor) after
each cleaning, keeping them cleaner for longer. Alternatively, keep
a spray bottle containing a 1:5 solution of bleach and water in the
bathroom and spray the tiles and shower screen every day.

To remove the white marks left by hard water on a plastic shower screen, rub with a used fabric-conditioner sheet.

Clean a shower curtain in the washing machine, adding laundry detergent and a little diluted bleach – instead of fabric softener – to the final rinse. Then dry, fully extended, on a washing line.

If you don't want to take your showerhead apart to unclog holes encrusted with hard-water scale, fill a plastic bag (making sure it has no leaks) with distilled vinegar, submerge the shower head in the liquid, secure the bag with an elastic band and leave overnight.

Banish mould and mildew and restore grouting to its former whiteness by pressing paper towels soaked in bleach onto the affected areas and leaving for as long as possible.

Soak tiles in neat distilled vinegar for 10 minutes to help
clean away hard-water marks.

Rejuvenate and polish tired tiles and whiten grouting by
spreading a thin paste of powdered wall filler and water over the area
and leaving for 30 minutes before rinsing off.

To clean enamel fixtures quickly, rub with a cut lemon.

Drains, Plugholes and Pipes

**Blocked plugholes and drains have all too predictable
consequences. These environmentally friendly suggestions
offer simple ways to avoid, and solve, inefficient drainage
and that tell-tale smell.**

To prevent drains and pipes becoming blocked,
make a habit of liberally coating the drain area or plughole with
bicarbonate of soda and then rinsing with boiling water. Do it at least
twice a month for best results.

If a drain is blocked, pour 2 tablespoons
of bicarbonate of soda and 2 tablespoons of distilled vinegar
down the plughole, putting the plug in while the mixture fizzes.
Then rinse with boiling water, and, if necessary, use a plunger.

Invest in plug strainers to prevent food remnants and hair
going down the plughole and blocking the pipes.

Effervescent tablets for upset stomachs work wonders on blocked
drains or plugholes. Simply crumble a couple into the hole before
rinsing through with distilled vinegar, waiting a few minutes
and then rinsing again, this time with boiling water.

Rinsing coffee grounds down the plughole helps to unclog blockages
in the short term; tea leaves will cause a blockage.

Tip the boiling water used to cook potatoes down an outside
drain – it will help to shift any lingering waste.

Windows and Window Frames

**Dirty windows, frames and ledges all detract from
the look of a room. These labour-saving suggestions will take
much of the pain out of cleaning them.**

Wash windows with the water left over from boiling potatoes,
as it leaves them gleaming. Alternatively, use a distilled
vinegar and water solution in a ratio of 10:1 to clean both
windows and painted window frames.

If you don't have time to wash the windows, remove grease marks
with turpentine before rubbing the glass with old newspaper.

Coat the window frame and sill with clear silicone floor polish as this
will deter dust from settling.

DIY

Do your dabbles in DIY end in tears, wonky lines and
spilled paint? Is your toolbox a disaster zone? If so, then take a peek
at these trade secrets and discover how the professionals
make it all look so easy.

Painting and Decorating

Painters and decorators can be very expensive, and many people prefer to have a go themselves. Here are some fool-proof tips to ensure and maintain a professional finish.

Are you having trouble removing remnants of old wallpaper? Once you have removed the top layer, spray it with distilled vinegar and leave for a few minutes. Scrape off the excess glue and then wipe off the remainder with more vinegar before rinsing with water.

To get rid of crayon marks on painted walls and paintwork, dip a dampened rag into baking soda and rub over the area. Alternatively, a thin application of spray lubricant removes all traces of crayon from painted walls, and can be rinsed off with soap and water.

If the paint is bobbling and flaking on a windowsill, water is probably getting in somewhere. Check the seals before stripping and repainting the affected woodwork.

To deter bugs and stop them sticking to the wet
paint when painting a room with the window open in summer,
add a few drops of insect repellent to the paint pot.

Line a paint tray with tin foil – it makes cleaning up at the
end of the day much easier.

Always stand a paint pot on newspaper or on
a paper plate if you are painting directly from the pot and
will need to move it around.

When painting the ceiling, cut a hole in a paper plate or
an old bath sponge and put it on your wrist to prevent drips
trickling down the paintbrush and onto your arm.

To achieve a clean, straight line when painting
cylindrical objects, such as chair and table legs, mark the level to
which you want to paint with a strip of masking tape around the
object and then paint up to the tape. When the paint is dry, remove
the tape and you'll be left with a neat finish.

If you lose the lid to your pot or need to cover some paint
which has been decanted into a smaller container during the day, use
an old shower cap or some cling film to cover the pot and
prevent the paint from drying out.

Avoid wasting paint if your brush is loaded at the end of
the day, or if you have to stop in the middle of painting, by wrapping
the brush in aluminium foil and putting it in the freezer. When you
need it again, simply take the brush out and leave it to defrost
before carrying on.

Place a dish of chopped onion in the room you are
decorating – it will help to get rid of paint fumes.

Look after your brushes. Clean as usual, rinse in water with a few
drops of fabric softener, and then secure the tip with an elastic band
when dry to keep the bristles in shape.

Transfer left-over paint into a smaller labelled tin, detailing the
manufacturer, colour and type. This way you have some on hand for
touch-ups and will be able to obtain more of the same colour
if you need it in the future.

Use a disposable razor to remove any paint that has spattered
onto the windows when painting sills.

Make sure you drill to the required depth
when putting up pictures or shelves by marking the drill bit
with a piece of masking tape.

Worried about banging your fingers when you hammer in a nail?
Try holding the nail steady with a wooden clothes peg rather than
your fingers for the first couple of blows.

To prevent your tools from rusting, place a moth ball in
the bottom of the tool box.

Keep small screws and nails tidy by sticking them
to a magnet.

Storecupboard Saviours

*A well stocked storecupboard will give you the power to clean
with ease, so here are a few of the best and most frequently
used grime busters for tackling the task of everyday
household hygiene.*

A-Z of Essentials
Indispensable ingredients for successful cleaning

Here are a few of the substances most commonly used in traditional household cleaning and stain removal. For safety, keep them away from children and pets, always follow instructions on the packet and handle with care.

Ammonia
Removes blood and fruit juice stains, and acts as a powerful cleaning agent. Gloves should always be worn when using this alkaline chemical, and good ventilation is essential.

Baby oil
Prevents grease building up on tiles and sinks and cleans stainless steel.

Banana skin
Great for cleaning shoes.

Bicarbonate of soda
Absorbs odours, cleans and is a gentle abrasive.

Biological washing detergent
Contains enzymes which break down protein and other stains.

Bleach
Multi-purpose disinfectant. Gloves should always be worn when using this liquid.

Borax
Natural deodorizer and disinfectant made from sodium, boron, oxygen and water. Gloves should be worn when using this powder.

Castor oil
Natural waterproofing agent.

Cat litter
Absorbs odours and liquids.

Chalk
Absorbs substances such as perspiration on collars.

Cinammon
Deters ants.

Distilled Vinegar – also known as White Vinegar
Can be used as fabric softener. Also is a disinfectant, neutralizes odours, removes limescale and grease and lifts stains.

Effervescent tablets for upset stomach
Dissolves and lifts grime.

Egg shell
Helps to brighten whites and make flowers last longer.

Glycerine
Softens and lifts numerous stains.

Ground coffee
Clears drains and lifts stains from dark-coloured carpets.

Hair shampoo
Gently cleans delicates such as cashmere.

Hairspray
Fixes stains such as ink and prevents them spreading.
Also deters flies and bees.

Hydrogen peroxide
Bleaching agent.

Lavender
Helps deter flying insects and perfumes laundry and rooms.

Lemon juice
Natural bleach and disinfectant.

Methylated spirits
Helps to dissolve stains.

Mint

Deters ants and mice.

Olive oil

Conditions leather.

Potato water

Brightens discoloured carpets, cleans glass and unblocks drains.

Rosemary

Deters insects.

Salt

Extremely absorbent and acts as a gentle abrasive
when cleaning.

Spray lubricant
Dissolves grease.

Talcum powder
Absorbent.

Tea leaves
Help to absorb odours.

Tea tree oil
Disinfectant.

Turpentine
Lifts paint stains.

Washing-up liquid
Concentrated soap which cuts through grease
and dirt and disinfects.

Temperature

To convert °Fahrenheit to °Celsius: (°F - 32) x 5/9 = °C

To convert °Celsius to °Fahrenheit: (°C x 9/5) + 32 = °F

°Celsius	°C or °F	°Fahrenheit
-23	-10	14
-18	0	32
-12	10	50
-7	20	68
-1	30	86
4	40	104
10	50	122
16	60	140
21	70	158
27	80	176

Length

1 inch = 2.540 centimetres   1 centimetre = 0.3937 inches
1 foot = 0.3048 metres   1 metre = 3.281 feet
1 yard = 0.9144 metres   1 metre = 1.094 yards

centimetres	cm or inches	inches
2.54	1	0.39
5.08	2	0.79
7.62	3	1.18
10.16	4	1.58
12.70	5	1.97
15.24	6	2.36
17.78	7	2.76
20.32	8	3.15
22.86	9	3.54
25.40	10	3.94

Distance

1 mile = 1.609 kilometres   1 kilometre = 0.6214 miles

kilometres	km or miles	miles
1.61	1	0.62
3.22	2	1.24
4.83	3	1.86
6.44	4	2.49
8.05	5	3.11
9.66	6	3.73
11.27	7	4.35
12.88	8	4.97
14.48	9	5.59
16.09	10	6.21

Speed

1 mile/hour = 1.6 km/hour
1 km/hour = 0.62 miles per hour

Area

1 sq inch = 6.452 sq cm	1 sq cm = 0.1550 sq inches
1 sq foot = 0.0929 sq m	1 sq m = 10.764 sq feet
1 sq yard = 0.8361 sq m	1 sq m = 1.196 sq yards
1 sq mile = 2.590 sq km	1 sq km = 0.3861 sq miles

Volume

1 cu inch = 16.39 cu cm	1 cu cm = 0.06102 cu inches
1 cu inch = 0.01639 l	1 cu m = 35.315 cu feet
1 cu foot = 0.02832 cu m	1 cu m = 1.308 cu yards
1 cu yard = 0.7645 cu m	1 l = 61.024 cu inches
1 gallon = 4.546 l	1 l = 0.219 gallons

1 US cup = 225ml

1 Australian cup = 250ml

Mass

1 ounce = 28.35 grams   1 gram = 0.03527 ounces
1 pound = 0.4536 kilograms   1 kilogram = 2.205 pounds
1 ton = 1016.05 kilograms   1 kilogram = 0.000984 tons

1 pound = 16 ounces   1 kilogram = 1000 grams
1 ton = 2000 pounds

Kilograms	Kg or Pounds	Pounds
0.45	1	2.21
0.91	2	4.41
1.36	3	6.61
1.81	4	8.82
2.27	5	11.02
2.72	6	13.23
3.18	7	15.43
3.63	8	17.64
4.08	9	19.84
4.54	10	22.05

International Dress Sizes

UK	Europe	US
6	36	8
8	38	10
10	40	12
12	42	14
14	44	16
16	46	18
18	48	20

International Children's Shoe Sizes

UK	Europe	US
6	23	7.5
7	24	8.5
8	26	9.5
9	27	10.5
10	28	11.5
11	29	12.5
12	31	13.5
13	32	1.5
1	33	2.5
2	34	3.5

International Women's Shoe Sizes

UK	Europe	US
3	35.5	4.5
4	37	5.5
5	38	6.5
6	39.5	7.5
7	40.5	8.5

International Men's Shoe Sizes

UK	Europe	US
6	39	6.5
7	41	7.5
8	42	8.5
9	43	9.5
10	44.5	11
11	46	12
12	47	13

GARDEN
Hints and Tips

Growing your own flowers, herbs, fruit and vegetables

can give endless pleasure whatever the weather.

This book offers ideas and advice to stimulate

your inner gardener, beat the blues of foliage failure

and help to combat the consequences of

environmentally unfriendly modern living.

Plants and Flowers

Flowers and plants can brighten almost any location in and

around the home, from colourful borders and creative containers to

indoor plants, window boxes and hanging baskets. Try these helpful

hints to ensure blooming success whatever the weather.

Garden Know-how

Gardening is a subtle combination of visual flair, scientific know-how, intuition and not a small helping of hard labour. Here are some general points to remember whatever your interest.

If you are to make informed choices about how your garden should look, you need to understand the changing face of the plot throughout the different seasons. If you have moved house, don't embark on a major garden re-fit for a year, so you can check what, when and where plants appear. Make notes and take photos (don't forget to date them) to help clarify your ideas.

Why not use a digital camera to record your gardening successes – and failures – through the year? Then you can keep a permanent record of your garden calendar on computer, together with notes to help you hit the highs – and avoid the pitfalls – in future growing seasons.

For a garden to succeed, it is important that the location and conditions are suitable for the plants and flowers in it. That means taking note of the weather conditions, the soil type and the direction that your garden faces. Soil testing kits are readily available from garden centres and are especially important if you're about to invest in a costly shrub or time-consuming crop.

In general terms, add lime to acid soil to make it more neutral and add peat moss, sawdust or pine needles to introduce acidity.

Buy plants only from outlets which obviously have the facilities to care for them. Trays of plants may look inviting on a garage forecourt but can you be sure they've been properly protected on cold nights? And are supermarket plants tended properly – getting the light and water they require – while they remain unsold on the premises?

Plants on sale in garden centres have usually been kept under glass. If they are destined to live outside, don't forget to 'harden' them off. That means giving them some protection in the open at first so they can gradually get used to more exposed conditions. Otherwise your purchase is likely to keel over quickly.

Native plants are more likely to thrive and survive than those imported from overseas.

Flower Borders

A successful flower border bursts with a riot of colour and vitality that fuels the imagination and leaves a lasting impression upon many budding gardeners. Achieving this effect in your own garden, however, is not always such a walk in the park. So here are some simple tricks and trade secrets for achieving chocolate box charm.

Don't ditch hyacinth bulbs from Christmas presentation displays. They'll never achieve the same glory in the pot again, but you can plant them into the border as an outside bulb. Remove the dead flowering heads, keep the compost from drying and plant out in April. They are happiest in the shelter of a tree or shrub.

Daffodil abuse is widespread – gardeners become irritated with the floppy foliage once the flower is gone and cut it back too early. Try, however, to resist the temptation to cut, tie or knot the leaves for about six weeks, when the leaves naturally fade, as they are still making food for the bulb to use in next year's growing period.

Plant a scattering of nigella or candytuft around daffodils
so their later spring growth will mask the daff's dying leaves.

It's vital to warm the soil before planting out new additions to
the border. You could use plastic sheeting or a glass cloche,
but canny gardeners simply chop up empty two-litre lemonade bottle
to do the same job. Just press the cut end firmly into the soil and
leave the bottle bottom or top pointing upwards. These mini-cloches
work well in pots too, and you can control ventilation by adding
or taking away the bottle top.

Grow extra plants to barter with friends and neighbours.
You'll get a wide variety at a fraction of the cost of those on sale
at a garden centre and you might pick up invaluable tips on
cultivation too.

There are internet websites devoted to plant swapping.
Use your favourite search engine and type in the name of the plant
you are looking for followed by the word 'swapping'.

Aquilegias or columbines are easy to maintain. They sprout
and spread energetically and are immensely decorative. But don't
hesitate to pop May or June-flowering plants in front of them to
hide tatty foliage when the blooms fade.

Grow sweet pea seeds in empty toilet-roll holders to encourage
a long, strong root system. The cardboard will not disintegrate
until the plant is ready to be moved to its final position.
Rolls of newspaper also make cheap, biodegradable pots.

It's best to plant in groups and in odd numbers. Three,
five or seven together always look more natural and less
regimented than two, four or six.

If you're planning a new border, mark out its proposed
dimensions with sand and 'shade' it in so you can get a clear
view of how it will look when complete.

Use boulders to flank a flight of steps. They provide the perfect
antidote to stark margins and an ideal environment for alpines
and low-growing rock plants that like their heads in sun but
their roots in shade.

Always tear – rather than cut – suckers off roses as near to the
base as possible. Cutting will cause the suckers to multiply.

Buy 'past their best' plants at garden centres when they
are on offer for knock-down prices. A bit of tender loving
care will invariably bring the casualty back to life.

Use the flower border as an extension to the vegetable plot by
planting decorative and delicious greens. A glance through the
seed racks will offer numerous choices. Chard, in particular, deserves
special mention, as it has a wonderfully pleasing form, comes in stalks
of striking colour and is versatile in the kitchen.

Don't dump fading pansies and violas. Cut them back hard
and new shoots should develop in a few weeks. This can prolong the
life of these cheery plants for at least a season.

Stylish garden borders often feature sculpture. However, these delightful focal points can be expensive to buy, so why not take a trip to the beach in search of your very own natural, individual and free ornament in the form of an interesting piece of driftwood, fashioned by the tides into an intriguing shape? Your one-off ornament will be a talking point and, if it loses its appeal, can be burnt on the bonfire.

It's relatively easy to chop down a tree but far more demanding to dig out the stump. So turn it into an unusual feature by digging in lashings of garden compost to enrich the soil and then planting frothy ferns at its base. If, in time, your stump is swamped by greenery, add in a few more logs of varying size from the wood shed to create your own 'stumpery'.

Indian summers can be difficult for camellias as they need water to form flower buds for the following spring. Make sure they get a soaking during dry autumns to prevent excessive bud drop.

Dry summer flowers to enjoy the blooms all winter long.
You need to plant suitable varieties in spring, including lavender,
Nigella, chives, *Monarda*, teasels, sea holly, golden rod and feverfew.
Pick in a dry spell after the dew has cleared but before midday,
choosing only perfect blooms. Hang upside down in small bunches
away from direct sunlight to preserve as much colour as possible.
If you want to collect seeds, tie a muslin bag around the bunch
during the drying process.

Rose cuttings are no more difficult to take than other
woody cuttings. In autumn, select several of this year's healthy
stems that measure about 25cm (10in). Cut below a shoot at
the base of each stem and above a shoot at the top, to eliminate
the growing tip. Remove all the leaves but two on each cutting,
plunge it into hormone rooting-powder, and then place with several
others in a large pot of gritty compost or a protected garden
trench. Water well and one or more of the cuttings should be
ready to plant out by the following summer.

Pick flowers in the morning, using a sharp knife rather than scissors or clippers, and place them in clean, tepid water out of direct sunlight. If you are arranging a mixed bunch which includes daffodils, don't recut the daffodil stems when you put them in the vase as they secrete a compound which can harm other flowers.

Hanging Baskets and Containers

Not everyone has a vast expanse of green outside the back door, but most of us have space for a few pots or baskets which, strategically placed, can make a potentially barren space somewhere leafy and special.

Don't skimp. A large, generously overflowing container has a much greater impact than a dozen small ones containing the same or a greater number of plants.

It's tempting to spread all the plants you have between the available containers. But it is worth keeping some back so that you can replace fatalities without additional cost.

Choose plants that match the proportions of the pot. Tiny alpines do not look at home in huge pots.

Prolong the life of a cracked garden pot by
circling its rim with strong wire, using pliers to twist
the ends firmly together.

Terracotta pots look sensational on a sun-baked patio
but they are always thirsty. Before planting up a terracotta or
clay container, soak it in water so it won't immediately
leach all moisture from the new compost. And consider
sinking terracotta pots into the border during hot summers
to prevent unnecessary water evaporation.

It is surprising how little moisture from a summer shower
penetrates a planted pot so don't rely on rain to water containers.
Make a habit of checking the container compost each day, no matter
what the weather, to be sure it's neither too dry or too wet.

Plants need to be watered only when the soil is dry to the
touch, so don't water by the clock. Always water in the morning or
the evening so as little as possible evaporates.

Try putting a couple of used teabags in the bottom
of pots and containers before you plant them up to help
to retain moisture.

Beware of those pots and hanging baskets where drought has shrunk
the compost in the container, as water will simply rush right past the
roots and out of the bottom, soaking your feet rather than the soil.
One solution is to buy compost with a wetting agent, which helps
break the natural surface tension of the water and thus makes it more
easily absorbable by the compost.

A simple, cheap and effective method of watering thirsty baskets is to incorporate a 2 to 4-inch empty pot in the top of the finished design. Add the water to this pot, and it will act as a reservoir to hold the water whilst it soaks into the basket.

Don't forget to feed hanging baskets. Regular watering is essential but the water running out of the bottom takes with it valuable nutrients which must be replaced if flowers and foliage are to flourish.

Containers can look wonderful but it takes a lot of effort to keep them in top condition. You can achieve the same effect by knocking the bottoms out of old or damaged containers and placing them on a bed of soil. The plants will root down into the ground and need much less watering in the summer months.

During heavy rainfall, prop containers carefully on their sides
so the soil doesn't become waterlogged and the crowns of the plants
don't suffer rain damage.

You can protect fragile plants from unseasonal frost by insulating
the container with bubblewrap and covering the foliage with
horticultural fleece or some old net curtain.

Add flair to a modern arrangement and enhance the colours
of the plants by using a coloured mulch, such as coloured gravel
or recyled glass chippings.

For shady spots, consider an all-green container display.
The key to success is using as many different types of foliage as
your budget will allow. Architectural palms, frothy ferns, grasses,
ivy, herbs and even conifers, grouped in different pots, can blend to
create a magnificently verdant effect.

Variegated leaves may be out of fashion with garden designers,
but they can help to lift a dull spot. Try the green and red *Pelargonium*
'Mrs Quilter' or varieties of colourful *Solenostemon*.

If you plant a container with scented flowers, try and position
it near a door or window, where it won't be knocked over, so you get
the benefit of its aroma indoors too.

Plant herbs in containers near the kitchen window so you can easily
reach out and pick the required herb whilst cooking.

For an unusual outside wall decoration, use a willow obelisk
as a wall-mounted plant basket. Line the upturned obelisk to
the halfway mark with moss, and then a discreet sheet of black plastic,
before filling with compost. Push the roots of your chosen plants
through the willow struts of the top half so that stems and flowers
will provide a layer of flora and foliage outside the obelisk. Top up
with moss and compost and plant up. Choose bright yellows, oranges
and reds so the obelisk becomes a flaming medieval torch.

Why not create a living house-number outside the front door?
Using a suitably sized pot, plant small echeverias to form the required
figure and fill the background with contrasting yellow
Sagina subulata 'Aurea'. Apart from an occasional trim,
it should be maintenance-free.

Houseplants

The lush foliage of a rampant houseplant brings the freshness of the great outdoors to even the smallest urban flat, while homes without greenery can feel like a domestic desert. Use these simple techniques for healthier, happier houseplants all year round.

More houseplants are killed by overwatering than neglect so resist the inclination to keep soil moist. When the soil appears dry, stand the pot in water for about half an hour, then discard any remaining water. A plant's need for water depends on its position and room conditions, so don't be afraid to use your own judgement.

Did you know that plants such as the spider plant, ivy, bamboo palm, fig tree and mother-in-law's tongue are all said to improve air quality? NASA scientists claim houseplants could help purify the air inside a space shuttle, so they are likely to be good for the home too.

If you mist or spray your houseplants on a regular basis, avoid using water from the tap, especially if it's known to be 'hard', as it may lead to white marks on the leaves. The alternatives are rainwater or boiled (and cooled!) tap water.

Uproot a snowdrop or two from your garden and wash off the soil clinging to its stem. Place the bulb and its root in shallow water and enjoy a long-lasting display of springtime splendour.

For some cats, the lure of a large houseplant as an indoor toilet is too great to resist. Make it altogether less attractive by keeping pierced lemons or oranges – or just their aromatic peel – close to the target plant and sprinkling the soil with black pepper. Cats find citrus and pepper a turn-off and would rather brave the great outdoors whatever the weather.

Sap-sucking insects, such as aphids and whitefly, often move in on houseplants and are happy to kill the host if they have to. Try washing an affected plant with soapy water, applied with a brush or a spray or, if the leaves are large, wiped clean. Small plants can also be dunked in a bucket. Rinse off any soapy water with clean tepid water. Resort to an insecticide only if that fails – no one wants to spray chemicals around the home.

Never place a houseplant on top of the television. It's usually too warm and often too far from adequate light.

Houseplants enjoy being outside in the summer for some refreshing sunshine and rainwater. But don't shift them into the garden too quickly as they suffer from night chills in a cold snap.

When you've run out of favours with the neighbours and no one
will water your plants while you're on holiday, try soaking the pots,
draining them and putting them into clear plastic bags.
Use sticks to fan out the plastic and make some air holes for
succulents. Secure the bags and leave the plants in their
mini-greenhouses until your return.

You can create a delightful gift by planting up an indoor garden.
Three-quarters fill a waterproof bowl with crocks and soil.
Then place a tall plant at the back, two bushy flowering plants in the
centre and a trailing plant in the front. It's best to split the plants once
the flowers have dropped and preserve them singly, otherwise
the roots become tangled.

On cold nights, take precautions with houseplants kept on the
windowsill by slipping a sheet or two of paper between glass and
leaves or, better still, moving the plants to a more protected spot.

Houseplants suffer a double assault in winter – dark days and central heating both put the plant under stress. To combat these factors, place a humidifier, if you have one, near the plants so they can enjoy its invigorating air flow. Or stand the plant pot in a tray of dampened pebbles so water evaporates upwards onto the leaves. Even when the soil is damp the leaves may be parched, so spray occasionally to freshen them up.

Production Zones

*Nothing beats organic, home-grown fruit, vegetables
and herbs, so whether you have a veg plot, an allotment, a
greenhouse or simply a windowbox, these trusty tips will help
you achieve the unmistakeable taste of green-fingered success.*

Vegetable Gardens

**The pleasure of picking produce from the garden
and serving it up just a few hours later can make hours of
back-breaking toil worthwhile. Certainly the flavour of home
produce is far superior to anything available on a supermarket
shelf. Here are some ways to take the labour pains
out of the veggie patch.**

To produce the best possible crop of seed potatoes, start 'chitting'
from late January. In other words, stand them blunt end uppermost in
trays (without soil) somewhere they can enjoy plenty of light. They'll
be ready for planting out when the shoots are about 2.5 cm (1in) long.

For a swift and rewarding remedy to a bare garden, try sowing
different types of lettuce. This humble salad leaf now comes
in numerous shapes, sizes and colours and will transform even flower
borders at speed. Although lettuce plants can be thinned, they don't
like being transplanted, so leave them where you start them off.

Don't plant seeds directly into the soil outside until the temperature is a steady 15°C (or 60°F). Hasty sowing puts the crop at risk.

Seeing a row of seedlings standing tall is always a thrill and makes the task of thinning out all the more heartbreaking. However, the most successful vegetables come from plants that had room to spread their roots and grow, which is why thinning – the unacceptable face of gardening – must take place.

Plant sweetcorn in squares of four or nine in a block. The system increases the plants' chances of pollination. If your flower border is big enough, pop a square in there too, as sweetcorn is ornamental as well as tasty. The plants need to be 35cm (14ins) apart so there's ample space to plant something in between. (Eat the cobs as soon as possible after harvesting as the natural sugars begin turning into starch the minute they are plucked.)

Fig trees grow well in milder climates, but be sure to contain the roots. A small bed no more than 75cm (30in) wide, or a large pot, are ideal.

Brighten your salad bowl this summer with the petals of edible flowers. Some of the most popular are nasturtiums, bergamot, borage, heartsease and pot marigolds. Most large seed companies offer packets of these easy-growers for home germination. Make sure you check before you eat: many plants and their flowers are poisonous, and you should never eat flowers which have been sprayed, including those from a florist.

Tie peppers to canes for support, and mist regularly to deter red spider mites. Once the plants start to swell, add a potassium-rich feed to the watering regime.

You can transform a plain wall into a vertical veggie patch
with a little DIY. Cover the wall with a wire mesh on timber
supports to provide a framework. Then attach pots and small
troughs securely with wire, making allowance for plant growth.
Use polysterene chips to provide drainage and reduce pot weight,
and choose miniature varieties of container vegetables such as cherry
tomatoes, aubergines, chillies, lettuce, basil and rocket.
Keep everything well watered. South-facing walls will do best.

If you spot blight on a potato crop you need to act fast. At first sight of the tell-tale black and withered marks on the foliage, cut off the affected leaves and burn them. The tubers below ground won't swell any further but it will prevent them from spoiling. Copper-based fungicides might save the rest of the crop but again rapid action is essential.

Grow your own new potatoes for the Christmas table by potting up 'second-cropping' seed potatoes, which have been treated to achieve swift growth, in August. In mild areas, the crop might succeed in open soil, but growing times will be quicker still if pots are brought into a greenhouse in bad weather.

Don't hang about when harvesting sweet potatoes. They are best pulled when the tubers are small and immature because even a slight frost causes damage. Have your garden fork at the ready at the first sign of wilting vines. Sweet potatoes can be stored for short periods in cool, dark places.

Seeds from home-grown tomatoes can last for ten years if collected and stored properly. Harvest when the tomatoes are at their ripest, then cut them in half and squeeze the pulp into a bucket. Leave the bucket in a warm place to ferment for three to four days. This process kills many diseases and breaks down the gel around the raw seed, which prevents germination. Add water, strain through a sieve, and rinse the seeds thoroughly before leaving on a plate for a couple of weeks, making sure you stir them frequently so they dry completely. Store in labelled, air-tight polythene bags in a cool, dark place.

Carrots don't need rich soil, as too much goodness encourages split stalks and root hairs. One traditional way of preparing soil for carrots is to spread fireplace ashes where they will be planted in the spring.

Give soil a nitrogen boost after harvesting beans by leaving plant roots in the soil after cutting off the stems to remove the dying foliage. The roots break down during the winter months to provide a rich source of nitrogen.

Don't trash leeks or onions that have gone to seed before snipping off the ornate flower heads. These can be dried inside the house and added to winter flower arrangements.

When harvesting spring and summer varieties of cabbage, cut with a sharp knife at ground level, and then score the top of the stump with a cross, to encourage a second crop.

Fill the 'hungry gap' in your vegetable garden with kale and sprouting broccoli. Both are ready in the early spring when there are very few homegrown veggies about.

Vegetable gardens need feeding for best results, but double-digging is history. Instead, spread manure over the empty bed in autumn and let nature do the hard work. By spring the frost will have crumbled it, the rain washed the goodness into the ground, and the worms will have tugged the remains below the surface. All that's left for you to do then is a swift turnover and a rake before planting up.

Different vegetables give – and take – various elements
from the ground. Employ a simple plan of crop rotation to keep
the soil from becoming pest-ridden or going stale. There are
many options but the simplest is to divide the plot into quarters
and in year 1 plant potatoes, celery and leeks in one section,
brassicas (greens) in the second, peas, beans and onions
in the third, and other root crops in the fourth. Rotate the
crops around the quarters in a four-yearly cycle.

Herbs

Herbs are plants that do more than tickle the taste buds. Planted separately in formal arrangements or among flowers and vegetables, they are attractive, aromatic and wonderfully versatile additions to the garden, which have the added benefit of being easy to grow.

Turn a raised bed into a scented seat by carpeting the top with herbs – thyme works very well. You'll have to check for bees before you sit though.

Try to site a herb garden close to the kitchen and barbeque to save yourself getting footsore in the summer months.

Don't plant fennel near dill or coriander. They will cross-pollinate and produce indeterminate, unproductive offspring.

Traditionally, the time to sow parsley is Good Friday, but most spring sowing should be successful. Don't give up on parsley seeds – they can take up to six weeks to germinate in a greenhouse or two months outdoors. And remember, parsley does better in full light.

Unless you want a garden full of mint, confine its root to a pot. There are numerous varieties and they look stunning grouped in terracotta pots. Other herbs that benefit from being pot-bound are bergamot, oregano and lemon balm.

Pop a bay leaf into the flour bin in the kitchen to keep away the weevil that thrives in flour stores.

When you run out of bubble bath in the summer, toss a
handful of mint into the water. Not only is its scent delicious
but it is said to soothe and strengthen the nerves.

Drying herbs for use at a later date will bring a touch of
sunshine and a reminder of summer to the dullest winter day.
Gather on a dry summer day, binding them together in small bunches.
Hang upside down in a warm, dry, airy place, out of direct
sunshine which will dull their colour, for several days until they are
dry to the touch. Spread the leaves singly on a sheet of cooking foil
and heat in a low oven for a short spell to complete the drying
process. Store in airtight glass jars. Remember: dried herbs have
a stronger flavour than fresh, so use sparingly.

Keep a potted basil plant on the windowsill to deter flies.
They hate its pungent aroma.

Strip the foliage from rosemary twigs to create
home-grown kebab skewers. The remaining hint of flavour
means they are especially good with lamb.

Greenhouses

Crops grow more quickly under glass than in the great outdoors, so households with a greenhouse can enjoy an early harvest. It's also a place of warmth and tranquility for much of the year, providing a cosy retreat for a break from outdoor gardening

Don't overwater seedlings in a greenhouse as they soon rot in the warm and wet environment. Also, avoid getting water on the stem of a seedling at the point where it meets the soil.

Many plants reared in a greenhouse won't get the benefit of visiting insects, so use a cotton bud or a paint brush to transfer pollen from one flower to the next. Repeat the process the following day.

When you run out of individual cells to rear seedlings, fill a seed
tray with compost and cover it with 1.3cm ($^1/_2$in) mesh wire.
Plant a seed through each hole in the mesh for even spacing and then
remove the mesh before growth begins.

Seedlings reared in greenhouses tend to get 'leggy' because
they have life so easy. Pass your hand or a piece of paper gently
across the seedling tops a dozen times a day to imitate a light breeze
and encourage them to stockiness.

When potting on seedlings, line the drainage hole with a
leaf so compost isn't washed away. The leaf will soon rot, leaving a
seedling with a strong root system that won't be disturbed
when you transplant.

To water thirsty plants – such as melons and cucumbers – in grow
bags, submerge an old plastic drinking cup with a hole in the
bottom next to each plant to the depth of the roots. Then simply
pour water into the cup and it's delivered where it's most needed.
And don't forget to cut drainage holes in grow bags to prevent
them becoming waterlogged.

Fit wire mesh to the lower sections of your greenhouse glass,
on the outside. You'll have some protection if you slip and fall
against the glass, and it acts as a football shield too!

Store any unused seed after sowing in a tin where it can remain cool
and dry, and packets should last for three seasons. That's a real
money-saver if you're planting just a little at a time.

If your dibber looks too big and clumsy to pot on
really fine seedlings in the greenhouse, use a cocktail stick instead.
Or transplant a small group of seedlings together.

Allotments

**Allotments can provide a sanctuary from the modern
world, a haven from the hubbub and an antidote to stress.
They offer an opportunity to flex your creative
and physical muscles – producing top quality, healthy,
organic food whilst gently exercising the body in a calm,
outdoors setting. Here are a few pointers to getting,
and keeping, an allotment the painless way.**

A full plot measures about 10 rods (about 9m x 28m or 30ft x 90ft).
If this sounds too much like hard work, inquire about
half plots. All local authorities have a duty to provide allotments
and most accommodate requests for smaller sites, although
you may have to join a waiting list.

The terms of the lease could curtail your activities
on the plot so study it carefully before you commit. There
may be restrictions on building a greenhouse, for
example, or planting fruit trees.

Check that the site of the allotment has a ready water supply.
No amount of tender loving care will make up for a lack of aqua.

Talk to allotment holders about their experiences on the site.
Night intruders – either human or animals such
as deer – may warrant the swift installation of defences.

Choose slow-growing, low-maintenance vegetables if you are going to be hard pressed to visit routinely a couple of times a week. Potatoes, onions, squashes and some beans do well even if pressures of work keep you away from the allotment for a week or two.

Standing on soil makes it compact and so less fertile. Stand on a plank when you are working among the veggies – it will distribute your weight evenly and avoid damaging the soil structure.

Save yourself unnecessary labour by covering unused areas with carpet or polythene sheeting. It may not look pretty but it's a great way to keep down the weeds.

Other allotment holders may be amenable to reciprocal holiday-care arrangements and to crop swaps when you have a glut.

Garden Maintenance

Gardens are fragile eco-systems and require watchful tending.
To maintain the natural balance, the right sort of pesticides
and fertilisers have to be correctly applied and pests of all types
need to be carefully controlled in as natural a way as possible.

Weed Control

Have you wimped out on weeding? Do you despair that, given the same warm, wet conditions, weeds shoot up whilst your cultivated plants slow down? You are not alone. Weeds are the single biggest factor in people giving up on their gardens. Luckily, there are many effective and easy ways to deal, and live, with these green invaders.

It sounds self-righteous but here goes, 'A little weeding every day helps to keep a big job at bay.' If you hoe little and often, it stops weeds before they get started and eliminates a potentially back-breaking chore. There's that other well-worn maxim too, 'Many hands make light work.' Bring your partner and any available children to the task.

Weed your garden in damp conditions. It's the only way the blighters give up easily, and it's a tall order to weed a patch of bone-dry soil and stay cheerful.

Invest in the correct tools for the job and weeding will become
far less of a chore. Daisy grubbers – a sturdy prong with a shaped
end – which will lift pesky plants from the lawn, roots and all,
are extremely useful, as are hoes and rakes, which can be used
to expose, uproot and kill young weeds.

Most weeds germinate in the top 5cm (2in) of soil, and
seeds that are buried any deeper rarely push through to the
surface. So avoid digging deep as that's likely to give life to
long-buried weeds.

The dandelion is a formidable adversary. Pour salt over the remaining
root once you've dug up as much of the plant as you can.

A cheap alternative to proprietary chemical weed killers is distilled vinegar. Once drenched in this environmentally friendly acid, a plant is swiftly pickled. For particularly tough customers, try heating the vinegar before applying it. A concentrated dose of salt will also sometimes beat the offender into submission.

Kill weeds with kindness – by introducing a programme of soil improvement. This works best against unwanted plants that prefer an acidic soil. Lavish quantities of compost and mulch will create the alkaline environment they hate and make it far easier to uproot the weeds.

Mulching deprives weed seeds of light and so kills them off. Although mulch is available at garden centres, why not use grass clippings, straw, newspaper, sawdust, black plastic, cardboard or even carpet? The more unsightly options can be disguised with a covering of chippings. Be generous. Mulch should be at least 10cm (4in) deep.

Compost needs to be generating a heat of over
60°C (140°F) to kill off intruder seeds, so make sure the heap is
functioning properly before adding weeds. It's safer to leave them to
rot in a bucket of water and then add that to the heap.

Don't add animal manure to the garden as it's likely
to be filled with weed seeds. Add it to the compost heap,
where they'll fry.

In the veggie patch make good use of green manure – a crop
that is grown simply to be ploughed back into the soil as fertiliser –
outside the growing season. It smothers the ground so weeds are
suppressed, brings nitrogen to the soil and can be dug in during
the spring to add more organic matter.

Twenty-first-century gardening is being shaped by a new tolerance of nature, and when it comes to weeds that means 'live-and-let-live'. The effort spent eradicating every weed might be better ploughed into cultivating a splendid bloom that detracts the eye from low-growing garden invaders. Some weeds are pretty, some weeds are helpful and some just happen.

Pest and Disease Control

There's nothing quite so demoralizing as seeing a healthy crop or beautiful bloom destroyed overnight. But don't throw in the trowel. There are remedies that keep the bugs at bay. Arm yourself with some effective tactics in the war of the garden pests.

Regular weeding helps to control garden bugs. Groundsel and sow-thistle, for example, harbour leaf miner, whose young burrow inside leaves leaving a white trail in their wake. Weed cover also provides the dark, moist environment that snails and slugs love to breed in, so clearance can pay off twice over.

Nematodes, a type of worm, are an expensive yet often effective biological control for slugs but they don't work well against adult snails, so be sure it is slugs causing plant damage rather than their shell-lugging cousins before investing in some.

One of the best ways to get rid of snails is to attract a thrush to your garden and provide it with a flat stone on which to smash their shells. Another cheap option is to lay an empty grapefruit skin on the soil to attract local slugs and snails. You'll be able to remove a small colony in one fell swoop. Shallow bowls or tin cans containing milk or beer are also irresistible to molluscs, who tend to topple in and drown.

Crushed egg shells, applied liberally around stems, will defend tender plants from snails at little cost without putting pets and wild birds at risk. This also helps to build up calcium levels in the soil. (For slug control, substitute eggshells with soot or sharp gravel.)

Construct 'steps' to allow frogs and toads easy access to a pond. Frogs, and particularly toads, are mighty predators of the hated slug.

To stop ants nesting in pot bottoms, cover the drainage hole
with part of a pair of old tights. If ants – and slugs – are
still a problem, pop the whole pot into the toe of a leg of
tights to halt their progress.

Ants can be a garden pest, not least because they herd aphids and
protect them. But, like most insects, they do have their benefits too:
if your soil is heavy, their activities can help to aerate it
and improve drainage, and they also help to distribute
the seeds of some plants.

Cut out small circles of cardboard or carpet underlay, snip
to the centre and lay them like a collar around the stems of brassicas.
This will halt the progress of the female cabbage-root fly as
she tries to lay her eggs beneath the plant. Any eggs deposited
on the cut-out circle will perish.

Use fine netting to cover cabbages, sprouts and so forth in the summer months. It will discourage determined cabbage white butterflies, whose grubs can strip a patch within days.

Are your broadbeans blighted with blackfly? Try planting English marigolds alongside the crop. The orange flowers are a beacon for hoverfly, which like nothing better than feasting on the blackfly. French marigolds, on the other hand, will help to ward off white fly when planted next to tomatoes.

To avoid disease and deter pests, ensure a row of carrots is fully covered by good-quality fleece from the moment they are put in the ground. Bury the ends in the soil so access remains impossible. If the sight of billowing fleece drives you mad, try planting coriander, onions or garlic to deter the damaging carrot-root fly.

Used coffee grouts laid down between rows of carrots will
help to prevent carrot rust.

Rhubarb leaves make an effective organic pest spray which is
harmless to bees and biodegrades very quickly in the soil, unlike
chemical sprays. Simply boil about 500g (1lb) rhubarb leaves in a litre
of water for 20 minutes using an old pan no longer used for cooking –
the leaves are poisonous and will both stain and contaminate the pot.
Leave to cool, strain and then dissolve 25g (1oz) soap flakes into
the solution. Pour into a spray bottle and label clearly, then keep
safely away from pets and children.

To deter most trunk-climbing caterpillars and insects, place a piece
of sticky tape around the trunk, about 50cm (20in) from the base.
Alternatively, try planting rue around the base of trees attacked by
aphids. Rue is said to transfer its bitter taste to the tree sap,
making it unappetizing to bugs.

Ladybirds eat aphids by the score and planting wormwood (*Artemisia absinthium*) will attract the red and black insects into the border for some early-season feasting.

Kill mealy bugs – small, white, cottony creatures – on houseplants by touching them with a cotton wool bud dipped in alcohol.

When choosing seeds, look for varieties that have been bred for pest resistance. 'Symphony' strawberries, for example, not only grow in all soil types and produce an abundant crop with an excellent flavour, but they also have some resistance to the vine weevil, while 'Lady Balfour' and 'Sante' potatoes escape unscathed from the double eel worm.

Spray mildew with a 9:1 solution of water and semi-skimmed milk – it's cheap and organic.

There's anecdotal evidence that copper wire threaded through a tomato plant stem in the autumn will arrest the progress of blight.

Avoid composting rose and tomato leaves. They can spread disease to next year's crops.

Coat the stems of chrysanthemums with petroleum jelly to halt the march of earwigs.

Cats can be a pain in the garden, but fortunately there are many ways to deter them. Try sprinkling a few drops of citronella or eucalyptus oil on some old tea bags and place them around the perimeter of your garden. To keep them out of your flowerbeds, scatter a few mothballs or coal-tar soap shavings among the plants.

Garden Safety

A day in the garden promises to be a relaxing, rewarding affair. Yet the great outdoors hides a host of hazards, and as many as one in five accidents occurs in the garden. Take note of the warnings below and make your backyard a safer place.

Whatever the weather, choose sturdy boots to keep your toes intact when mowing and digging.

Full-length trousers are a wise choice, and use tough gloves for heavy-duty chores like bramble-clearing. The thin variety don't offer enough protection from thorns.

Use rubber gloves when handling garden chemicals. Measure out only as much as you need and keep the rest safely in its original packaging so you have the instructions next time you use it.

Store chemicals in a locked, frost-free cupboard out of
reach of children and pets.

Don't maintain an uncomfortable position for hours during weeding
or you will suffer severe aches and pains the following morning.

You can make your own kneelers from old baby-changing mats
or roll mats used for camping. The latter are especially good as they
are long and you won't have to move them so often.

You should always make sure you use plenty of sunscreen,
wear a hat and drink a lot of water when gardening in the
glare of the sun. This helps to prevent dehydration and the nasty
headache which can accompany it, as well as protecting against
sunburn and sunstroke.

Assess any garden task before embarking on it. Can you manage it alone? Put the job off until help is at hand if necessary, or you may risk the long-term health and strength of your back and other vital joints. Always bend from the knees when lifting heavy weights.

Decorative cane tops designed to prevent sticks from poking into eyes are available from garden centres – at a price. Economize by making use of corks, ping-pong balls, potatoes and even the teats from feeding bottles. Just about any soft stopper will do.

Plant sap dries hard on secateur blades if it's not wiped away immediately, and this inhibits the action. If you've neglected the blades in this way, bring them back to form by applying white spirit with a scouring pad. And don't forget to oil their moving parts several times during the season.

Slate paths turn into skating rinks after spells of ice and frost,
and even a short, sharp downpour can create a skidpan. Replace
with alternative materials along main routes and use the
slates for ornamental purposes.

Scatter bonfire ashes on frozen paths and driveways to reduce
the risk of slipping while on foot or driving.

Even a puddle poses a potential threat to toddlers.
Children have been known to drown in as little as 3cm (1in) of water.
If you have youngsters, or some are visiting, ensure containers are
emptied after rain showers and buckets are upturned.

Garden clutter has a habit of lurking in corners and, given half a chance, will multiply like bacteria. It's hard on the eye and can be a hazard. Tedious as it seems, good gardeners clean up as they go along. That way they avoid unnecessary trips and slip-ups.

Learn to identify poisonous plants or you could end up cultivating a killer. The biggest threat is poison ivy, which is luckily still rare in Britain. Many domestic plants, however, are toxic or an irritant. Beware of foxgloves, laburnum, heracleum (or hogweed), castor oil plants, yew, oleander, deadly nightshade, autumn crocuses, lily of the valley and aconitum. Fortunately most poisonous plants taste unpleasant, but always be wary of berries that look succulent, which could have a disastrous effect on your stomach and nervous system.

Garden tools are rich pickings for thieves. One insurance company calculates that gardeners suffer an average loss of £135 every time their shed is burgled. But there are precautions you can take. Each item can be marked with your postcode, for example. This not only deters crooks but also ensures stolen property is returned, if recovered. Contact your local police station to see what services it offers. Assistance will almost certainly be free of charge.

Around the Garden

Most gardens are made up of distinct areas, each requiring

different care and attention. These can range from man-made

structures such as patios and paths to lawns and natural

areas where wildlife can take refuge.

Patios and Paths

Even the best-tended plants need a framework to display them at their finest and provide safe access. This is where patios and paths play their part, as cleverly designed hard landscaping can alter the perspective of a plot, dividing it into distinct zones or making it appear larger than it actually is.

A patio doesn't have to be attached to the side of the house. It is far more important that it is sited in a sunny and perhaps secluded spot.

Mistakes in planning paths and patios are costly and time-consuming to correct, so gather as much advice as you can before laying a slab. Use cardboard squares cut to scale to plan and model a path or patio before you buy any paving. That way you'll avoid either spending too much money or finding you have too few slabs.

A patio is only as good as the foundation it's built upon and that should be 10–15cm (4–6in) deep. Skimp on the base and the patio will quickly deteriorate.

Tables and chairs that constantly wobble are a real pain. To achieve a level finish, choose brick, paving or even terracotta tiling rather than cobbles or gravel.

Reclaimed brick is a popular choice for patios. But beware of bricks with a high salt content because they will crumble quickly. Many bricks are fine for the task but the wrong variety would mean disaster, so inquire before you buy.

Gone are the days when it was wise to choose large tiles
rather than go to the effort of laying small ones. Diminutive
slabs are now available on a roll, with each secured to its
neighbour on a wire mesh. Be aware, however, that the rolls are
heavy and make patio projects a two-person operation.

Avoid using white, or predominately white, stones to
cover large areas of patio or pathway. On sunny days the reflected
light can be painfully bright.

Wall-to-wall paving can look monotonous so incorporate a
few gaps at the planning stage. You can fill them with cobbles, gravel
or some low-growing plants – thyme is ideal. If the paving is
already in place, why not lift random slabs to vary the texture?
Do weeded patios and paths result in too many unforgiving lines?

Why not plant up the cracks? If there's enough soil beneath
the slabs and the climate is generally kind, try the houseplant
mind-your-own-business with its appealing, rambling habit.
To survive hot weather, look for drought-proof plants such as
woolly thyme, or self-seeding plants suitable for the conditions.
If you are short of soil, the humble moss may be enough
to soften the area.

If you are creating a path through the garden, try to make it wide
enough for a wheel-barrow – or you could spend years ploughing into
borders as you clear debris from other beds.

If you're installing a hot tub, surround it with decking or
paving rather than gravel or you could find that the tub seats quickly
become peppered with stones.

Lawns

**Achieving a perfectly smooth expanse of immaculate,
emerald green lawn remains for most of us a distant dream,
as our plots and ambitions are constantly thwarted by one
or more of the three principal pests – weeds, animals and
children. Don't despair, however, as there are some simple
measures that can help make your vision a reality.**

Treat mower blades with spray lubricant at the beginning
and end of the season. It improves the cutting action and makes
cleaning a breeze.

Does your lawn suffer from moss invasion? Don't just reach for the
box of chemicals. Upright mosses indicate acid soil that could benefit
from a dose of lime. Trailing mosses flourish where there's poor
drainage and that might be solved if you give overhanging branches a
haircut. Some forms are even encouraged when you cut lawns too
closely. Identify the cause and you'll save money and time.

Did you know that a weed can produce as many as
250,000 seeds a year? It makes sense, therefore, to mow before
the weed heads bear fruit, so you can stop a whole new generation
of weeds from taking root in the lawn.

To help control moss, reduce disease, strengthen growth and
give the lawn a lovely bright colour, apply lawn sand, which contains
iron sulphate.

When you are sowing a new lawn, be sure to use seed that is
guaranteed weed-free, or years of frustrating labour will take root
alongside the new grass.

Light rain provides the perfect conditions for using lawn
feed as it prevents scorching.

Try to avoid using nitrogen fertilizer as autumn approaches.
It can make the growth soft and disease prone.

It's difficult to predict when the last lawn cut will take place.
If it's too close to the first frost, then it could spell disaster for the
grass. So don't forget to raise the cutting height of the mower blades
at the end of summer to prevent subsequent lawn damage.

Worms are the gardener's friend – they help to break
down organic material and aerate the soil – so simply brush unsightly
worm casts off the lawn with a besom rather than kill the worms.

If you loathe your lawn for all the hard work and heartache it gives you, why not turn it into a wild-flower meadow? You don't even have to grub up the existing grass – simply introduce seeds or install plug plants from reputable domestic suppliers to the existing grass. Aim for about 85 per cent grasses and 15 per cent wild flowers – avoiding rampant ryegrass. For spring flowering, choose primroses, cowslips and yellow rattle, and for summer go for harebells, common knapweed and field scabious. Then all you have to do is mow once a year after flowering to keep the grasses in check.

Green Gardens

We now know that excessive use of man-made substances is harming the world we live in. As we reject the quick-fix solutions that rely on harmful chemical aids, it's time to turn again to the commonsense ground rules that generations of past gardeners relied upon.

The lifeblood of a garden is compost, and fortunately it's easy to make your own. There are no hard-and-fast rules, but it is advisable to site your heap, bin, wire-mesh container, open-topped wooden box or tumbler in a distant corner of the garden. To make rich, nutritious compost, you can use any number of vegetable items, which will heat up together and rot down to a dry, crumbly, rich brown medium. Other popular ingredients include grass cuttings, weeds (without seed heads), peelings, pet bedding and leaves. The most dedicated add nail clippings, hair and even urine. Don't add meat scraps or four-legged scavengers will take an interest. Experts say it's best to layer items, but even if you don't you will in time produce nutritious compost for little or no cost.

A day spent choosing seeds in the garden centre
in the depths of winter can be a wonderful tonic. But for free seeds,
try collecting them from your own garden. The time to harvest
is when the flower head is dead and drying. Store the seed in
food bags or clean margarine tubs, not forgetting to label them,
and then treat as you would commercially bought seeds.

Spread the ashes from a wood fire or bonfire around plant bases –
they are rich in potash and double as a slug deterrent.
But don't use ash from a coal fire as it will kill off plants.
It's best saved for the foundations of paths or patios.

Scrub and save wooden lolly sticks to use as plant markers. An old
venetian blind can also be chopped up to provide useful tags.

Don't toss away tin buckets, cans, old baths, plastic tubs or saucepans. With luck, they'll already have a lived-in look and, laden with blooms, will be full of cottage-garden charm. One enterprising publican turned an abandoned Ford Fiesta into a planter/talking point. Remember to drill drainage holes where necessary.

Take pride in being a 'second-hand Rose' and reap benefits in the bank as well as the garden. Garage and car-boot sales often yield cheap garden tools in sound condition. You should avoid electrical items though, as faulty products could pose a potential hazard. You can also scoop up statuary, bird baths or troughs at architectural salvagers or antiques fairs.

Peat bogs are an over-plundered resource, and gardeners are the main target customers. You should, therefore, avoid buying peat, or compost containing peat, especially as experts say it can be satisfactorily replaced by a number of products, including coir. It may cost a little more in the short term, but in the long term it will help to cut the cost of the environmental damage to the landscape and wildlife which inhabit the bogs.

Protect tender, newly planted seedlings with a plastic collar cut from the body of an empty plastic lemonade bottle. It acts as a draught excluder and a slug and snail fence. You can cut at least three collars from every 2-litre bottle.

Put spare guttering to good use inside the greenhouse by suspending it to provide an aerial plant holder. It is slim and sleek, easy to water and makes welcome extra space at busy times.

Economize on the use of water around the garden by installing a water butt that will conserve rainwater for dry days. Liberal mulching around thirsty plants will also save a can or two and help keep the nation's water table healthy at the same time.

After hard-boiling eggs, cool the pan water and use it on thirsty plants – it's full of minerals from the eggshells. The cooled water from boiled vegetables and the fish tank is also a bonus for plants in containers.

Use old tights as ties around the garden. They are perfect for
securing the fleshy stems of tomato plants.

If you get a fragile parcel through the post, don't
ditch the wadding. Bubble wrap can protect pots and the
plant roots in them from frost.

Use discarded supermarket orange and lemon nets to store bulbs,
dried onions and even garlic. Thread string around the ripped opening
to draw the ends together and then hang on a hook.

Wildlife Gardens

**Watching wild animals and birds flitting about the garden
can be at least as pleasurable as seeing young plants flourish
and bloom. And it's a compliment – a sign that an ecosystem
is at work – when wildlife is at home in your garden.
Here are some tips on how to embrace nature.**

Don't prune or move shrubs and hedges at nesting time. You'll be
depriving birds of a home in which to raise their young. Put off the
job until late summer when the fledglings have flown.

Insects are nature's pollinators and every garden needs a broad
spectrum of our six-legged friends to thrive and survive. Keep bees,
wasps, butterflies, hoverflies, moths and ladybirds happy by planting
corn marigolds, pot marigolds, broad beans, borage, buddleia,
night-scented stocks, nasturtiums, the poached egg plant, Californian
poppies, sunflowers and sedum. Make sure you water them during
droughts or nectar production will grind to a halt.

Simplicity is key in the wildlife garden, especially in the choice of flowers. Double-flowering varieties look exotic and extravagant but they are bad news for insects, who struggle to penetrate the more complex flower heads. Stick to single-flowering types at least some of the time.

Include a wild area in your garden so nature can provide for itself. Nettles, for example, are a vital food source for the caterpillars of native butterflies, but are largely eliminated from tended gardens.

If you use a chemical spray for pest control, apply to blighted plants at night to minimize the risk to pollinating or predator insects, which won't be around in such numbers as in the day.

For short spells in the spring and summer, it is helpful to
keep birds off seedlings and crops. Try making your own low-impact
bird scarer using ribbon or tinsel on sticks. You can also tie tin cans
closely together on a piece of string so they crash together in a
breeze. Or put up bells, kites or even make your own scarecrow.
Remember to take down the device as soon as the crop is harvested
or you risk the birds becoming familiar with and contemptuous of it.
Alternatively, stake out a seeded area with twigs and then wind wool,
cotton or string between them to make a homespun net.

Consider putting up wildlife lodges in your garden to give
animals and beneficial insects the best chance of happy life.
Lodges are available for ladybirds, lacewings, bumble bees, bats,
hedgehogs, dormice, fieldmice and birds ranging in size
from tits to owls. There are also butterfly feeders – just add
sugar water – and boxes with an integral spy system that offer an
inside view on the resident's activities.

Keep bird baths topped up during dry spells. And moisten crusts before adding them to the bird table to help keep birds hydrated.

When installing a bird table, enclose its supporting post inside a piece of plastic drainpipe about 76cm (30in) long so that predatory cats can't easily climb up it. If you are making your own bird table, another simple deterrent is a small circular platform placed just below the one intended for feathered visitors.

You can fill a new pond with tap water if you leave it for two weeks before adding foliage or fish. Ideally, a new pond should have a couple of bucketfuls of water taken from an existing pond to get the benefit of valuable micro-organisms that will give it a natural head start.

Any food left in the pond five minutes after feeding time should be removed with a net. Uneaten food will rot, pollute the water and put fish stocks at risk.

Beware the sleeping hedgehog during autumn clean-ups.
It is likely to hide away in bonfire piles and might
lurk under leaves that you approach with the sharp and potentially
lethal prongs of a fork.

Leave flower heads on teasels and sunflowers at the end of the
growing season. They are not only hauntingly beautiful but
provide a valuable food source for birds.

Gardening Glossary

Garden-speak sometimes sounds like a different language. Use this basic guide to get a new insight into gardening techniques.

Annuals Plants that die off after their growing season and have to be replaced.

Biological controls The introduction of living things, including nematodes, predatory midges and parasitic wasps, to control or eliminate garden pests.

Biennials Plants that complete their life cycle in two years.

Bulbs Perennial plants that have an underground food storage system.

Chitting Laying seed potatoes budding side up in an egg box or seed tray without soil, and leaving in a warm light place until they have sprouted roots.

Cloche Transparent plant protector made of glass, plastic or fleece.

Companion planting Putting different plants side by side to assist in organic pest control.

Cordons Single-stemmed trees trained along a wall, trellis or knee-high fence.

Cuttings Making new plants from old by taking a section of stem, root or leaf and placing it in soil or water until it grows its own root system.

Double digging Digging to the equivalent depth of two spade blades.

Earthing up Loosely covering new shoots with compost in early spring to protect them from the cold.

Layering Method of plant propagation in which the stem is stripped of leaves and pinned into soil. When it develops a root system it can be severed from the parent plant.

Mulch Cover for soil.

Nitrogen Essential element of plant food that prompts healthy growth.

Pergola A framework of wooden beams providing a sheltered walkway or seating area.

Perennials Long lasting plants with flexible root stems that die down in winter and grow again each year from hardy roots.

Phosphate A fertiliser with phosphorus that helps fruiting and root formation.

Potager A decorative veggie patch dating from Tudor times.

Potash A fertiliser containing potassium, which helps plants use sunlight for growth.

Scarifying Removing moss and debris from the lawn by rake or powered scarifier.

Take Five for...

The following lists of 5 plants are grouped to give you a few ideas of the varieties which are suitable for different locations and types of soil. So, whether you want to create a bold, brightly coloured border, a pleasantly perfumed patch or simply an eye catching window box or container display, these top tips will help to ease the indecision at the garden centre or when buying on the internet and start you on your way to green-fingered glory.

A Tropical Border

Canna 'Durban'

Lobelia 'Tupa'

Dahlia 'Bishop of Llandaff'

Kniphofia Caulescens 'Red Hot Poker'

Ricinus Communis 'Castor Oil Plant'

An Acid Soil

Azaleas

Rhododendrons

Camellias

Ericas

Pieris

A Clay Soil

Acer plantanoides

Amelanchier lamarckii
(snowy mespilus)

Ribes sanguineum
(flowering currant)

Roses – most varieties
but check the label

Philadelphus

Annuals

Alyssum
Antirrhinum
Delphinium
Impatiens
Verbena

A Shady Spot

Hostas
Hellebores
Lilies of the Valley
Impatiens
Evergreen ivy

A Scented Garden

Tobacco plant (white)
Honeysuckle
Jasmine
Sweet peas
Lonicera

A Container Garden

Camellias

Abutilon

Cordyline

. *Cistus*

Lavender

Alpines

Aubretia

Gentiana

Oxalis

Saxifraga

Silene

Trailing plants for Window Boxes

Chlorophytum (Spider plant)

Trailing Fuchsias

Hedera (Ivy)

Nasturtiums

Lobelia

Flowering Shrubs

Fuchsias

Cornus (Dogwood)

Prunus

Rhododendron

Mahonia